Missing Persons

Missing Persons

Hilary S. Jacqmin

WAYWISER

First published in 2017 by

THE WAYWISER PRESS

Christmas Cottage, Church Enstone, Chipping Norton, Oxfordshire, OX7 4NN, UK
P.O. Box 6205, Baltimore, MD 21206, USA
https://waywiser-press.com

Editor-in-Chief
Philip Hoy

Senior American Editor
Joseph Harrison

Associate Editors
Eric McHenry | Dora Malech | V. Penelope Pelizzon | Clive Watkins
Greg Williamson | Matthew Yorke

Copyright © Hilary S. Jacqmin, 2017

The right of Hilary S. Jacqmin to be identified as the author of this work
has been asserted by her in accordance with the
Copyright, Designs and Patents Act of 1988.

All rights reserved. No part of this publication may be reproduced, stored in
a retrieval system, or transmitted in any form or by any means, electronic,
mechanical, photocopying, recording, or otherwise, without the prior permission
of both the copyright owner and the above publisher of this book.

9 7 5 3 1 2 4 6 8

A CIP catalogue record for this book is available from the British Library

ISBN 978-1-904130-87-1

Printed and bound by
T. J. International Ltd., Padstow, Cornwall, PL28 8RW

for Dave, my sweetheart

Acknowledgments

Grateful acknowledgment is made to the following publications, in which some of these poems first appeared:

AGNI Online: "Fat Man"
The Awl: "The Girl Detective," "Sideshow Banner: The Engagement of the Fat Lady and the Pocket Man"
Best New Poets 2011: 50 Poems from Emerging Writers, edited by D. A. Powell: "Wedding Album"
concīs: "Oven Timer"
DIAGRAM: "Drunks," "Jughead, Mid-Life"
FIELD: "Atomograd"
The Hopkins Review: "World's Fair"
Measure: "Homewood, 1816"
MINERVA: "Advertisement, Architectural Supplement to *Country Life*," "The Grand Tour," "Ladies' Maids," "The Last Country House"
Passages North and *Oxford Poetry*: "Day of the Dead"
The Raintown Review: "The Hunting Horns"
Subtropics: "The Trial"
32 Poems: "Coupling"
Unsplendid: "The Greenwood," "Ode to Our Magister"
The Urbanite: "Charm City"

Some of these poems were written under the auspices of an O. Ruth McQuown Scholarship Award from the University of Florida.

Thanks to my writing teachers and mentors, especially David Baker, Michael Hofmann, John Irwin, David Leavitt, Eric LeMay, William Logan, Peter Markus, Padgett Powell, Jean Reinhold, James Thornton, Sidney Wade, and Greg Williamson.

Profuse thanks go to V. Penelope Pelizzon and Philip Hoy, who offered invaluable editorial advice and shepherded this book to publication, and to my kind and talented friend Michael Levy, who shot my author photo.

Acknowledgments

Thank you to all my poetry cohorts and fellow workshop participants at Johns Hopkins University and the University of Florida. Special thanks go to Andrew Donovan and Natalie Shapero for helping me shape earlier drafts of this book.

Thanks to Betty and Joe Walters, Adele Travisano, and Dennis Hale for all of the evenings of poetry and good company.

Thank you to my longtime Shaker Heights friends, especially Sarah, Cat, Colette, Ike, Jake, Susan, Owen, Holly, Andy, Grayden, and Sam, as well as Ann, Chuck, John, Jane, Zanna, and David. Thank you to my Alpha Delta Phi brothers and sisters and their commitment to coeducation, literature, and *Buffy the Vampire Slayer*.

And, finally, thank you to the Novek, Jacqmin, and Fishman families, especially my parents, Maxine and David Jacqmin, my sister, Laura Jacqmin, and my husband and first reader, David Fishman.

Contents

Skull and Toad   13

I

The Hunting Horns   17
Rabbit-Proofing   18
World's Fair   20
Ode to Our Magister   22
House-Hunting   24
The Greenwood   26
Sex Ed   27
Blues for Tom   30
The Breaking Wheel   33
Wedding Album   35
The Army Bride   36
Employee of the Year   38
The Press   40
Man-eater   41
Lotus Beaker, 1st c. AD   43
Coupling   44
Oven Timer   45
North Shore   46
Drunks   47
At Seventy   49
Arcadia   51

II

Day of the Dead   55
A Personal Narrative of the Indian Mutiny, 1857   56
The Grand Tour   57
Ladies' Maids   58
Advertisement, Architectural Supplement to *Country Life*   60
Animal, Vegetable, Mineral   62

Contents

Homewood, 1816	63
The Last Country House	65
Food Editor, *Electricity on the Farm* Magazine	66
Livia da Porto Thiene and Her Daughter Porzia	67
Sabbathday Lake	70
The Girl Detective	71
Winter Quarters: Cleveland, 1960	72
Charm City	73
The Trial	75
Letter from Algiers Naval Station, Louisiana	77
Jughead, Mid-Life	78
Dust Bowl: The Advance Man's Geography	80
Sideshow Banner: The Engagement of the Fat Lady and the Pocket Man	81
Showman with Performing Bear in the Westerwald	82
Fat Man	84
Atomograd	85
Paradise	88
A NOTE ABOUT THE AUTHOR	91

Skull and Toad

Mitsuhiro (1810–1875)

Miniature skull. Miniature toad.
    Mitsuhiro carved them
    in the diminutive
from a walrus peg, posed toad,
    his eyes like lumpfish roe,
against skull's hairline suture.

Are *netsuke*—kimono toggles—
    memento mori, or their opposite?
Hey pal, at least you're still alive.
    At night, toad pants, a dry, sarcastic ghost.
Skull's hollow grin, in profile, recedes
    from cranium to golden wishbone.

Are skull and toad best friends?
    Or do they prefer
    the perfected Octopus
Grasping a Piece of Coral?
    They're like reluctant partners
in some buddy flick dubbed into Japanese.

I want to pin them—Skull and Toad,
    Rats on a Daikon Radish,
Mass of Sea Creatures,
    even Child Frightened
By a Mask—beneath my burnt tongue.
    I want to eat the full-on Edo Period.

Something as precisely-hewn and tiny
    and as dentine-shiny
    as a human tooth
must be a working charm.
    It may not save my life,
but then again, like a woodcut peony

    sizzling with ants, it might.

I

The Hunting Horns

When father bought a battered single horn
from the termite-riddled Antique Mart
on Mayfield Road, we feared his brain
      had sponged inside the slide-grease jar of his skull.
    Most men his age took up eccentric hobbies
of a different sort: sloe gin, hot rods,
or divorcées. My father screwed
      his Farkas mouthpiece to the pipe and blew—
      such tinned, half-fretful notes, the lamplight winced.
Poor dad: an aero-acoustician,
born with a clingstone ear; the physics
      of the exponential bell evaded him,
      although his *Wunderkammer* swelled with instruments.
His double horn—a Conn 8D,
restored—bayed out the mournful overture
      to Handel's "Water Music" like a hound;
      three rotors in his nickel Yamaha,
his brass collection's only splurge,
froze up. He left it coiled on the buffet,
      a lacquer nautilus reflecting mother's
      strung-up lusterware: chipped plates inscribed
with speckled hinds and fireback pheasant hunts,
each captive scene transposed, then flayed.
      Years passed. When we could bear no more, we sank him
      in the cellar, perched on a Hepplewhite chair,
spit valve and practice mute in hand,
lips pursed in swollen embouchure.
      Scales startled from his horn like wayward quail.

Rabbit-Proofing

Sure, the rabbit was soft.

Soft as unpunched sourdough,
her yeasty chest rising
in the wet, astringent litter
of the wire hutch.
No custard-apple heart
beat sweetness through
her musky veins;
no deeper thought starred
behind her petrified stare
and thrashing kicks
but hindgut escarole and estrus.

What *didn't* our rabbit ruin?
She pissed the dogwood lap
of my silk nightgown
into yellow shantung.
Her pastry-cutter incisors
abraded mother's mock-
antique sampler pillow.

We finally understood
why my school-friend's father
butchered their English Spot,
serving the marbled meat
as *hasenpfeffer* one Sunday afternoon,
then stretching the herringboned pelt
over a high beam in the garage.
It was an act of righteousness
and overcoming all things rabbit:
that urge to mark and cower
that lies in each of us.

Rabbit-Proofing

Our rabbit was a fierce, bad toy.
For two savage months,
the nutmeat of her hard shit
piled behind sofas and stools
while we all thought *pet shop*

and *murder, murder, murder.*

World's Fair

"You have to be prepared at any moment to face difficulties and even dangers by knowing what to do and how to do it." —*Agnes and Robert Baden-Powell,* The Handbook for the Girl Guides or How Girls Can Help to Build Up the Empire

Girl Scout Troop Fifteen, bused from Akron-Canton,
wore Hawaiian skirts, passed out virgin Mai Tais,
and lei'd the Daisy scouts with raw frangipani.
But *we* were stuck, each year,

playing Panamanians. Puzzling isthmus,
only our bouffant-coiffed troop leader, Barb Ross
(ex-missionary), loved your canalled shoals. Land bridge,
middling child, wish-

bone snapped off and jammed in the Pacific's throat,
home to meatball vendors and pork pie hats, we
hated you. The Brownies from Peninsula
Village, last canal

town in Summit County, nabbed Holland three years
running (tulip *speculaas*, *klompen*, and windmills
littered their Delft booth). Even Berea, HQ
of suntanned Cadettes,

hooked the USSR: exotic, gulag-
pocked, a second homeland for Ashkenazi
on their way from dance hall bat mitzvahs. I know
Juliette Gordon Low,

rice-punctured eardrum ringing, would be ashamed
of the scowls we shot at banana republics.
Our Cuyahoga apathy spanned the Western Reserve.
Dust films my handbook;

the badge for Celebrating People's peeling
off my jade green sash. Now, nation-building's
news again. The foreign girls grow more foreign.
They recede, eyes veiled,

into some vast Bedouin distance, or slip
through tidal locks in an imperial barge,
radiantly shrouded, inscrutable scouts
on an unknown mission.

Ode to Our Magister

God bless Bob White, whose first-born son, convinced
he was Odysseus's hound, barked, shook loose
his golden curls, and licked his old man's shoe.
How gently Mr. White, that Monte Bianco
of a man, his tits like glacéed chestnuts, swiped
the putto's head with Sunday's furled *Plain Dealer*.
Our Latin teacher lacked all classical
proportion. His skin was marbled Parma ham.
His hair was blond, chaff pulled from ancient cereal.
Athena only knew how Mrs. White,
who taught Pythagoras's theorem down
the hall, could bear to touch that shrouded gut.
It seemed heretical to picture him,
a happy nude, sprawled *in flagrante*
on an Alban grape-embowered *lectus genialis*,
not just because the mind's eye wept to conjure it—
our noble *magister* blanched at the barest hint
of sex. Catullus, in Bob White's softcore sixth
period translations, turned literal and flaccid
as a textbook out of *Mr. Chips*. Stammering,
Mr. White reluctantly allowed that Lesbia's
pet bird could symbolize some masculine part,
a rousing organ with a proper name—
he beat his palms together in remorse
at such a crass confession. *Fiddlesticks!*
In truth, it was a boon to know there'd be
No rides!, per pedagogical decree,
for bright young things in Mr. White's sedan
while panpipes bleated from the stereo,
no late-night Dionysian orgies masked
as AP study breaks, no civil suits.
Bound by the words—*Semper ubi sub ubi*—
the secret lingo (*always wear underwear*)

Ode to Our Magister

of Orphic mystery, we metamorphosed
into acolytes, each pupil primed, in strict
devotion to an antique temple's rites,
to sing of chalk-streaked arms and of the man.
Our Palatine. Our Pantheon. Our Rome.

House-Hunting

Because he was indifferent to the Browns,
the Buckeyes, golf, and candlepins,
but minded that our breakfast nook was dim;
because he liked to peer at studs
and other people's astragals, and knew
the worth of travertine; because,
a blueprint carpenter turned engineer,
he missed his putty knife and awl;
my father's only sport was real estate.

He sought out fixer-uppers: bungalows
with avocado wall-to-wall;
cramped ramblers perched on scenic overlooks;
or Cape Cod cottages whose stairs,
though rickety, were orieled with light.
Perhaps the mansard roof was split,
the bedrooms more like badger dens, the back-
yard overrun with katydids—
my father didn't mind. He looked beyond

the birds-of-paradise that flocked some lived-
in living room and glimpsed good bones:
load-bearing walls enforced with high-speed steel;
partition walls which, multiplied,
could stretch a kitchen's skeleton until
it ached with plasterboard. His mind
a helix nail, my father saw, unseen,
each painted architrave that housed,
in miniature, the house's pin-drop heart.

House-Hunting

The perfect fixer-upper never showed,
although one sunken gablefront
in Pepper Pike came close. Our center-hall
Colonial fit father best,
so we stayed put. He built a new garage,
bumped out the dining room and deck,
and planted sour cherry trees. The house
expanded like a star magnolia.
His soul, expansive, topological,
was rigged, like louvered blinds, to let in light.

The Greenwood

for Emily

As Rosencrantz our junior year,
you traded A-line skirts for slacks,
slipped off your tea rose tights and sheer
silk cami, tied loose tendrils back.
Beneath the footlights' green leaf smear,

you'd flush, a crushed, half-wild rose,
your hair a tangled crown of thorns,
rose cut, despite your rakish clothes.
Small wonder Hamlet wavered, torn
about that missive. Still, he chose

to send it, sealed, skulls sketched along
the edge—*memento mori*, death's
bleached souvenirs. Ophelia's song,
her herbal litany and breath-
less suicide, seemed to belong

to byzantine, mosaic states.
We lived in trellised Shaker Heights.
Our homes were Tudor gray. Our fates,
spun out through Clotho's endless night,
gleamed: green, suburban, bantamweight.

They found you in December, rolled
inside a Chinese rug. You had
been dead for weeks: your corpse slabbed, cold
as winter and rough weather, clad
in rosebud Mary Janes, a gold

cross, bent. Your eyes, burnt brambles, stared.
We dreamt that you might rise again,
like ice storm roses given care,
earth, sun, shocked rain—but death's domain
beat back that kingdom of the air.

Sex Ed

Mr. McIntyre
warned us, his voice
a pocket square soaked
in motor oil: the modern world
was made of rape
and murder.
                In the Value City
parking lot, strange men would
Super Glue our sedan locks.
        They'd slide beneath
those cold car bodies
and wait to slash
our coy ankles.

Other men might
cop a corkscrew feel
on the Big Dipper,
        or press a pistol
to our tube tops
on the Superior bus.
        The lesson there was
Don't get off the bus,
like we were Rosa Parks
in the diminutive, driven
not towards action
        but away, our body politic
so apolitical
we could barely snap
our uncrossed legs shut. Solo peril,

then, was nearly
everything: a vacant
packing plant; the ungloved
hands of the orthodontist;
Nirvana, boyfriends,
or a Baby Ruth. It was

Sex Ed

        the sawdust down
on a young girl's clavicle,
the way her stomach
swelled like durian.
Picture a water birth lit
        like a snuff film.

Mr. McIntyre straddled
his chair and leaned
        in closer, his cheekbones
straight razors. Before
this gig, he'd been
a sad male model. Still almost
diamond-cut as Tyson Beckford
or the slopes at Boston Mills,
        he gazed at us
like we were already dead:
Ladies, for your own good,
        scream. You've got to move
like Crisco on a griddle.

        But most of us would not
be raped in dead malls
or grocery stores. None
of us would be discovered
hot-boned at the Parma
Gem & Mineral Show.
Of course we'd never taste
tasteless Rohypnol;
we'd never even
leave Northern Ohio.
        Instead, at forty, we'd throw
our backs out, or miscarry again. Work
wouldn't pay. Our shrinks

Sex Ed

would raise their rates
and shake their heads. Why didn't
anyone teach us

that we'd lose
> our balsam health,
> our equipoise, well before
we lost our breath? Or that
our adult lives would mean
not the smudging-out of purity, but
> an endless progress
towards our orphaning—dead
mothers, brothers flattened
from Vicodin or spastic bowel,
fathers irradiating
in cramped oncology wards?

Our terminus was
> something like Elyria:
flat, unstoppable, an endless sprawl.
> We could scream until
> we tasted blood, scramble,
unsnap our bodysuits,
or grab a fire iron from the wall—
> it didn't matter. Soon
our bodies, male
and female both, wouldn't
be our bodies, and the quarter moon
would rise like a machete.

Soon the filmstrip of the Cuyahoga
would catch fire. Then, thank god, we'd sleep.

Blues for Tom

Tom Hagan's got
a crush on me.
He wants to take me out

on the Zamboni
to clean the ice.
Tom Hagan smells

like gasoline and sharp grass
and swimming pools.
His work uniform

is blue as the smoke
rising from LTV Steel, blue
as a Parma girl's

eye shadow
or the moon-bruise
blued around her eye.

I half want to touch
his craggy mouth,
that sandy hair gophered

under a tight blue
Indians ball cap
day after day. I almost want

to hold his face, that
twenty-six-year-old kid's face,
his sweet sad-veined hands.

Tom Hagan is
the biggest mistake
I'm never going to make.

Blues for Tom

But if this were
some dream I'd let him
take me anywhere.

I'd stud sapphires
through my two cold ears
and drive downtown

to the Flats,
to the big blue Cuyahoga,
and sit and drink

Bombay gin with him
at a river bar
that never closes.

I want it to be
inevitable. I want to be
the kind of girl

who'd hold him—
or who wouldn't
be afraid. I want

to sit beside him
in the Zamboni
after everyone has left,

ice powdered through the arena,
our faces shining
lazuline or aqua

in the glass,
hard carved hearts,
the mirror ball setting up

Blues for Tom

its spin and "Blue Velvet"
playing, marine notes cut
and pulled through the air.

We won't be dancing;
we won't even be talking
much. I want

love to be that
unthinking, that calm
and without error,

as blue and still
and stoppered
as Lake Erie in the winter.

The Breaking Wheel

The bastard thing of dating is the boys
who take you bodily to the Renaissance Fair,
how they are all inexplicably named Ashley,
and how they encourage you to chaw
on turkey legs as leathery as blackjacks.

In bare October, when you are wan with homesick,
you'll accept the smoky torture show, the juggling school
that smells of tainted milk. Still, you'll feel a righteous,
virgin anger when you spot his paunch, and almost gag
when he fondles the gold breast of his pocket watch.

You are eighteen, and want to be both pacified
and dazzled. You have barely heard of Goldschläger,
but you've seen it as the motes of sawdust in a slender
woman's eyes. I'm telling you to turn away
from your knight errant's recap of his planet-crushing novella.

Pretend to listen to another dim madrigal. Go quick, before he takes
your hand. In the mud somewhere, outrageous people bridle ponies.
This fairground is stamped absolutely flat, as brown
and unassuming as a crushed potato skin, and all around you
jousting, or the pantomime of jousting, thunders on.

Oh lady, heartsick, foolish, and unbeautiful,
today, you want the fake hangman to be a real
friar swinging a rosary. But even sunlight is obscured
by the bigness of quasi-medieval popovers, and boys
are something you'll just have to stomach—their

boisterous stubble or toad shyness, their mercuric
pimples, the fact that some of them major
in computer science, a deader language,
you think, than Latin. Still, you will not be some Ashley's girlfriend.
Idiot wenches may think that they are princesses,

The Breaking Wheel

but you believe in dust, a cut hoof, *Troilus and Cressida,*
and terrapin. The way crowds shrink magic
like a microscope, so that it becomes
a lantern slide. Words like "Terpsichore";
the taste of lanolin. Already, you are back in the college van

for an hour ride, being lectured about star clusters,
the memory of the sham White Stag and the imposter Globe
and the sorry tilting fields devoured by locusts
rising inside you. You possess a terrible new knowledge
of the existence of Morris dancers. Must everything, even

courtship, be badly reenacted? In your mind, it is the real
Renaissance. You are tied to a Catherine wheel, quite terribly
tormented. But bittersweet will come, and
all the other bodily metaphors: frost and flame,
heartsick, heart's ease, the wounded wrist

of the beloved. Even the gypsies who cannot read
a single palm know you could not be fooled
by anything less than complete heartbreak.

Wedding Album

You say "I do" on the Main Street Lot, beneath
the span of Brooklyn Bridge. I clench my teeth
and fake a Miss America grin as you,
my ex, become conventional, a True

Romance case study in lace and vintage pearls,
my last lost cause. I think of the gamine girls
I kissed in college—Pantene-haired, tattooed,
their skin scrubbed raw with tea tree oil—such crude

replacements. You smoked Troyas, championed Ayn Rand,
sang backup in a Bowie cover band
from Latvia. My senior year, half-drunk
on single malt and boxed white wine, we sunk

onto the loveseat at your grandma's house.
As "Modern Love" blared, I undid your blouse
and fumbled with your Maidenform, unsure
of what came next, too flushed, too amateur,

to run my hand up your tanned legs. I played
the novice that brief summer: a secret, staid,
and steady girlfriend. In August, you returned
to school. You dated—*men*, you wrote. I yearned

for you for years. At your wedding reception, I sign
the guest book. Beside my name, I scrawl *Be mine*.
I hide out in the rented photo booth,
feeding rolls of tarnished quarters in. The truth,

I know, is that you're gone for good, a wife,
quite happily domestic. Only my life
burns out. The camera flashes, catching my face
in every washed-out frame. My features blurred. Erased.

The Army Bride

The night you call me from Fort Hood
I cinch my cherry rickrack apron tight
and leave a fryer popping on the stove.
"Hey, Laura Ashley. I'm so tan,"

you brag. "My butt is bronzed. The sun's
the one good thing about Texas." I picture you
belly-down on your waterbed, kiss curls
bobbed with Comanche Pool chlorine,

painting your nails Oil Slick or Smog.
"I'm bored," you moan. "Jake's been deployed
to Bagram. He always cooked, so now
I'm living on Nutella and Tex-Mex."

You don't know anyone, "except
some rednecks from the Temple typing pool
who aren't into early Kung Fu films."
Your neighbors—well, you bought a Glock.

At night, you tiki-torch the living room,
balance an Afghan scimitar on your hip,
and belly-dance. You've nailed snake arms
and camel rolls. Last month, you scored a gig

at some Moroccan dive near Waco.
"No shit," I laugh, and crack a Pabst, then chug.
"Three hours, sixty bucks, plus all the grape leaves
I could eat!" The blackened chicken's black;

it blisters in the frying pan.
"If you drive down, we'll stone crab on the Gulf.
Or I'll move up and room with you. You'll love
my harem pants. They're coin-flecked. Semi-sheer."

The Army Bride

"Some day," I murmur. Fingers crossed.
"I'm just so fucking lonesome here," you sigh.
In my cramped kitchenette, the smoke alarm
is going off—a roadside bomb you barely hear.

Employee of the Year

I lasted two weeks at the bakery
before they took away my keycard, smock,
and walk-in freezer privileges. I spilled
the orange curd, hacked trays of gingerbread
into mutilated squares. My linzer hearts
hemorrhaged raspberry jam. My boss, JoAnn, claimed,
when she let me go, that it was nothing personal.
They'd hired a dishwasher-slash-prep cook
on the cheap, some skull-tattooed ex-con who ran
the Hobart while he frosted coconut cakes
one-handed.
                To supplement my teacher's wage,
I spent one winter as a bookstore clerk,
steering *Gossip Girl* aficionados toward
The Ruby in the Smoke. My measly paycheck
went back into books, from Dorothy Draper
to *Bad Cats*, but my wrapping skills were woefully
sub-par. The owner shook his head and said,
in time, I'd learn to scissor-curl. He canned
me once the Christmas rush died down. Inside
my car, a turquoise Ford with busted heat,
I gripped the steering wheel and cried until
the Jones Falls blurred.
                Next fall, on Beacon Hill,
I worked as the attaché to a miniskirted editor.
Legs made me dust her first-edition *Pentagon
Papers*, rejected every foundling manuscript
I pushed, and hissed, behind closed doors, that I
was lazy, lacked true grit, and probably should pack
the publishing world in and go to J-school
on my parents' dime instead. Flinching, I fled
her Greek Revival lair.
                But worse, perhaps,
than these mundane humiliations were the jobs
that stuck: the teaching gig at an unaccredited
pre-K where ADD kids gorged on Teddy Grams

Employee of the Year

and where I fished two bloody nickels out
of Sarah Banker's ski jump nose; a hot
career as a data entry temp at Unitor,
recording ship fire safety stats (three life
rafts, fourteen cylinders of CO_2)
for Russian hulks with names like *Askold Star*;
two years as a proto-Junior Leaguer, feet stuffed
into navy pumps, my mouth cinched in a nervous grin,
performing dutifully each small task (the tumbler
of mineral water fetched, the expense reports
fudged) demanded of my office by the plutocrats
and priests who kept our tiny college floating
on a chummy tide of fellowships.
                                        To know
you cannot worm away—that this cramped desk
will be exchanged for other desks, not rooms
with views, each rolltop stretching on until gold watch
retirement, the saline drip, and then the lily wreath—
and that each company and corporate hack
has seized some shred, however partial, of your listless soul—

I see it now: those early firings
when I slipped, shivering, off the sunken hook,
were really favors. *Too late now*. At night,
I cook my supper—steak *au poivre* with peas—
and eat it over lurid episodes
of *Law and Order: Special Victims Unit*.
On TV, all work seems just, inspired.
This bottle of wine won't drink itself, I think,
and pour myself another glass. Not until
this *Côtes du Rhône* transforms back into grapes,
then wild vines, denuded of all labor,
will I be free to take my rest.

The Press

The church of work is bracketed by mid-
Atlantic rain. Our stockpile
of Constant Comment wanes.

Copyediting my life into an ampersand
so everything is & and & and &.
The pressure of my redline shaves

each subtle point into an hourglass of sand.
So I am more or less anonymous.
My heart's a cubicle half-built from books,

and marked-up page proof rubricates
my hands to rust. Someone else's blues
and galleys, some hot scholar's drive.

My soul's lukewarm, a cooler
bubbling up, the cockroach pinned
beneath a colleague's coffee cup.

The break room's just the final period
on all our run-on sentences, and life's
eternal errands pale beside a tower of Fall 2000 catalogs.

This is my tenure and my monograph.

Man-eater

She cornered me at the copier to gloat
about blind dates in oyster bars, the suits
(investment bankers, Swiss economists)
who Amex Black'd plateaus of *fruits de mer*,
two dozen Bluepoints mounted, belly-up,
on mounds of diamond salt, or blinis flecked
with Tsar Imperial, then ringed with snails.
She flirted with each Gucci'd money man,
downed double g&t's in Back Bay walk-ups,
flashed a little or a lot of leg, but, braless,
cinched in strapless silk, resisted bedding them.

She porked the King of Kosher Meat instead.
"The Jews," she bragged, "at least, the Hasidim,
think I'm some loose Sephardi, vanished from the tribe,
the kind of semi-shiksa you show off
to Rabbi Gold. I keep reminding Max
I'm just a Spanish girl from San Jose
who can't tell *tzitzit* from *kasha varnishkes*,
but he's convinced, I shit you not, that we're
swept up in some postmodern *West Side Story*. Did
I mention that, on our third date, I cooked
him shrimp and grits, with bacon grease? He licked
the Wedgwood clean."

                    Quasi-heroic, too,
was each pedestrian disaster she relayed
in hyperbolic tones: her papillon,
that epileptic mutt whose piss destroyed
a parquet floor; her stolen Mazda, stripped,
stuck up on blocks, a kind of blessing: no
more parking tickets! Each tragedy took a month
to tell, but, even working overtime,
half-numb from hunger, I couldn't wait to hear
the next outrageous narrative. Her verve,
her braggadocio (her ex-fiancé

let her keep the princess-cut engagement ring),
was awe-inspiring. She spun those tales
like some low-rent Scheherazade, as if
her life depended on the arc. She'd storm
in breathless, late, her fitted suit an eggplant gleam,
and spill her guts: blow jobs, blown job interviews,
or porterhouses black with truffle butter,
it was all the same to her, an equivalence
of passion.

        She works for Light & Power now—
some office straddling a strike-slip fault.
When darkness falls, I hear, it barely strafes her.
Divorced, remarried, seven months along,
she play-acts all the smutty bits in *Cock
and Bull*. She's equal parts cracked solitaire
and scored *torchon*, still digging on her knees
for something missing: a stack of naked Polaroids,
a secret wedding band. Always finding it.

Lotus Beaker, 1st c. AD

Green-gold ewer, glistered with rust,
so what if I've forgotten every conjugation
but *amo, amas, amat*? In school,
I loved a woman with quarried feet
and Roman sandals. Like me, she was
an exile from Latin class. When she went
to 80s Night in a makeshift *stola*,
spelt curls pinned back, her hips
an archeology of motion, it hurt,
how much she looked like Ceres:
both ancient and unforgiving,
those eyes the color of threshed wheat.
So I gave up on harmonizing with her
to "Total Eclipse of the Heart." Instead, for years,
I slept in longing's cold colosseum.

Lost love's the bevel of this beaker,
worn down lip by lip; it's the bulbs,
those simulation lotus buds, that smother
the glass, cracking into rainbow. These days,
I'm drawn to eyesores from Herculaneum:
still barges and Suburban Baths,
each sub-baroque body ashed to statuary
by some indifferent lover's cigarette.
I've finally learned that love, returned,
is fine as charcoal fixative—or maybe
it's the halo of Greek fish sauce around the moon.

Coupling

In Somerville, we rented out
a double-decker's second floor:
scuffed hardwood, listing balconies,
a built-in china hutch. We mixed

our silver, cataloged our books,
and spiked the butcher-block with knives.
I bought a bruise-blue hyacinth
that died within a week. At first,

we fought when he was out of work.
We fought whenever we were late;
or working late-night, overtime;
or when I used the kosher wok

to stir-fry prawns with mustard greens.
So shacking up meant overdue
electric bills, commuter trains,
the boiler stuttering off, black ice,

and brownouts, clasping sweaty hands.
He'd fill my vintage limeade glass
with gin each time the level dipped.
We shared a grease-soaked paper bag

of onion rings, hands pale with salt,
as constant as New England snow,
then watched the float-glass windows cast
an iceberg on our bedroom wall.

Oven Timer

A bakelite timer
        forged
like a flocked hen

surveys the gas range
        in this pre-war kitchen.
A mahogany biddy

that clucks off seconds;
        fat bantam
of the dinner hour.

Our broody Buckeye
        orbits,
a bell suspended

in her belly.
        See her
pea comb, rosy

as the errant pearl
        of blood
that punctuates an egg.

North Shore

Those Cambridge weekends, bored
by office boilerplate,
the works and days of slush,
and every stalled commute

to Harvard Yard, we chipped
my sea-glass Ford from its
eternal snowbank. We took
1A to Wonderland,

past Greyhound Park's defunct
dog track, past burnt-out bars
and factories embalmed
in ice. Our industry

was dying, too. Each public
beach and pie shack urged
us north to Marblehead,
where yacht clubs bent like birch

and saltspray roses lined
the crest of Windmill Hill.
We came too late to crash
the Philanthropic Lodge,

to tour the Old Spite House
or bid on spinnakers
and fake antiques. Instead,
in ice-cleat Lands' End boots,

we'd tread the granite split
between Old Town and New,
two wind-lashed privateers,
our coupled and uncoupled fears

as fierce and tenuous as love.

Drunks

The ones who switch to seltzer
are all younger than you:
twenty-five or thirty, thirty-two.
At parties now, they chain
smoke, muscular as Christ,
their faces lit like end-

of-spring bonfires. Before
they sobered, there were broken
hands, sand, blackouts, and
the kind of sex that's more
like throwing up. And yet,
they are so lovely now:

tan refuseniks, both men
and women glistening
in a way that lightfoots,
slowly sipping Rex Goliath,
never do. Teetotalling
has, somehow, saved them, kept

their minds like buffalo,
their heartlines luminous
as mariners' maps, while you,
the photo-finish of
rib-eating innocence,
get fat, not blitzed, on beer.

You're old, or getting there.
The world's unfair: the zodiac's
a lie, and every problem drunk
you eyed in college—punk
or labor activist,
pre-med, post-goth, classicist—

Drunks

has shaken off that sheen
of fake rebellion on the way
to real, grown-up despair.
They could not help themselves,
they couldn't stop, and so
they quit. What's *wrong* with you,

that you should ply them now
with drinks that—honestly—
you don't know how to mix?
You almost miss the cool,
reflective chip of ice, the way
your first martini spilled,

and watching wasted boys
perspiring, their eyes
like tacks: they couldn't, wouldn't, watch
you back. Does safety mean
that someone's got to be
impaired? If someone must,

let it, at long last, be you,
mouth blurry as a shot
of Snap, your confidence
some perfect ping pong
volleying through an extra stout,
your beer gut softly beautiful.

At Seventy

After she lost the weight—all of it,
evaporate—my mother swore she was as slender
as she'd been on her wedding day. Perfected.
    Then one day, she was even thinner.

And though her illness wasn't fatal,
    her bangs fell out, the bright old
        rooted carrot of them gone to ivory wire,
which hurt (she winced) her beauty.
I felt her wrists all over with malt-fatted hands;
they were brittle as the chicken bone candy
she'd sucked on as a child. Now, her knuckles snap
    like a command. And when she smiles, her teeth
        are yellow ice, her molars coined fillings. Forgive me

if I miss my mother big and freckled as a harvest moon,
her stomach its own Russian immigrant, coasting
into our business-minded Protestant home.
    I loved her melting milk-jug profile, her only flatness then
the flats (her "dainty dots") from TJ Maxx
    that scuffed light from the maple floor.

When I trace her spine now, each nodule stands out: the skeleton
breaks through like diamonds. She is the living woman
    and, simultaneous, the ghost, more tenuous and compacted
than she has ever been, her muscles
    useless as the silver acorns in the story
of the magic nut-tree. Sooner now
than I had guessed, I will inherit all her antique rings,
her pin-bottle of violet perfume pooled
and stinking like chewing gum, the tarnished badge
    from her Atlantic High sorority, even her first husband,
        that jealous shutterbug I never met: all those halved
        and thinning memories.

At Seventy

I see her clearly now, in ground. Her old flesh
like butter: clarified, then gone.
Her soft nose. Her tears for us, or because of us, when we
were cruel, calling her "piggy," calling her "bitch"—and then
when she was cruel right back—oh, all that mean passion,
    just destined for the grave.
Like slamming all the doors and slamming all the doors again
    meant that we could ever bear to lose her.

Arcadia

Even before we were cast out (sunburnt, naked)
    into the unholy cities of the Fertile Crescent,
we stayed up late, tattooed with starlight,
    wondering about God: If He had seeded
this paradise garden for us, why
    were the paths so compulsively raked? Why—
in that *locus amoenus,* where rain steamed
    the leaves of the wild ilex open
almost unconsciously—were trailing roses forced
    to bloom in needle-thin parterres? The devil,
hissing in the glass cactus of my ear,
    insisted, "All this rigid botany,
the symmetry of *qanat* rills and fresh-
    mown cyclone grass—it means Our Father's love
for you depends on your obedience."
    It was not enough for Him
that we loved the moon (earthshine and albedo),
    that we worshipped the pomegranate-stung sunset
or the hot dung He'd packed to build our walls.
    On the last day, God called *us* the con artists.
What could even He do to mend such willfulness?
    He shook His head and told us about torn sutures,
about unswept ashes and snow blindness,
    about the beards of foreign men, about women's hips
curved like wine bottles: the world we'd made. Then we were
    in that world, weeping blood. Sometimes I think of us
before we fell: tan and hungry, like teenagers
    skinny-dipping in some suburban pool,
our terrible sincerity, our bodies
    as whole and as beautiful
as they would ever be, and all around us
    the curious sugar palms bending towards
the water, flexed and inconsolable as ribs.

II

Day of the Dead

The Peabody Museum of Archaeology and Ethnology

On All Saints' Day, when hammered darkness peels
    the layers of the underworld
apart like gold, the corn-smut dead come back.
    Parched cartoon bones, they scull Divinity
and scale the Peabody with chalkstick feet,

    drawn in by desiccated sugar skulls
and crumpled marigolds that glow like quince:
    our *Día de los Muertos* detritus.
Beneath *papel picado* skeletons,
    they mill around the Hall of the Americas,

inspecting the pottery of their lost lives.
    They miss mezcal. Like us, they love sweet bread
inlaid with sesamoids, and washed-out Polaroids
    of relatives who drowned on honeymoon.
Abandoned by their dog's-breath psychopomp,

    their husked-tamale prayers go up in smoke.
They are the lonely dead, electric stiffs.
    We living are the ones with second sight,
the seedbank in the locked Herbaria.
    We give our mottled light to everything.

A Personal Narrative of the Indian Mutiny, 1857

after Anna Madeline Jackson

In early June, just after morning prayers,
while we sat eating coddled eggs and toast,
the Sepoys marched on Seetapore. They killed
our pets in the garden: two spotted deer brought up
on milk; Barbary goats; my talking myna.
The natives rushed the Commissioner's bungalow,
shot Mr. C, beheaded Mrs. C.
Remember when, as Bluebeard's found-out wife,
she wailed "And will you cut my head off, husband"?
She slumped on the veranda like a cow.
Mountstuart and I escaped into the jungle
while Minié balls, like skirling bagpipes, droned;
they burst the Club's gin bottles into stars.
My brother had to trade his Lucknow sword
for elephant chappatis dripping ghee;
his pistol went to Parsees, for showing us
the way. At night, the golden jackals howled.
From far away, we must have looked like punkah-
coolies squatting in the soporific dirt.
Our sunburnt skin grew brown as jaggery;
we wrapped our hobbled feet in mango leaves;
I'd stripped my muslin skirts a month ago,
to ford a cataract. I thought about
nearsighted Georgie, darling sister, lost
to us, most likely left for carrion.
Would heaven be as hot as India?
I pictured speared-through memsahibs afloat
on clouds like tattered parasols, and Raj
commanders drinking bloody quinine rickeys
at the celestial Club. One day, I woke
to see a total eclipse reflected in
a washing-tub. When the midday sun returned,
we heard conch shells and tom-tom drums start up.

The Grand Tour

At Kew, she clambers up
the nautilitic stairs,
past Permian cycads
tethered to the trusswork,
past swaybacked *Coco de mer*,
each seed lobed
as a suffragette's rump.

Suspended from
the coldshear canopy,
she gazes through
Darjeeling light
at transplanted raffia,
fronds that swelter
against the steam-ground glass.

Her mute hands fox
the jutting trunk
of England's oldest potted plant.
Against the lawn's vast map,
a gilt pagoda shivers
like a cutthroat eel.
All empire has come to this.

Ladies' Maids

Upstairs, they like us
artless, virtuous,
and thin, our skin
as pale as soda ash.

We learn
from one another
how to compound laudanum
or counterfeit perfume.

We wield
our tortoiseshell
tongue-scrapers
with practiced hands.

Our Scots vulgarities evaporate:
the poxed child, roaring,
the husband lost
in some provincial cow pond. Better

to say, "The infant seized
with smallpox cries"
and "He was drowned,
but it was long ago."

We know a little French,
but not too much.
We know the names
of all the major tragedies,

and how to rub
the soot from soiled furs.
We hold our tongues.
We never flatter anyone.

Ladies' Maids

All day, we dress
our mistresses, re-dress
or undress them. Our hands
grow tea-gown smooth.

Summers pass. Pettish,
we slip up, boiling
the goldfish water,
severing a too-tight ring.

In the indifferent light
that fills our downstairs cells,
we sit idle, our hair unbound,
wearing last season's

cast-off frock, considering
our inheritance. These days, we look
like someone else, perhaps
the lady of the house.

We know the shape
of her tight ribcage.
We've grown into
all her oldest things.

Advertisement, Architectural Supplement to *Country Life*

May 4, 1912

I.

At Auction: Coping Balustrade,
Italianate, from Trentham Hall,
each heavy post a half-
grown pomegranate,
        plus thirteen hand-turned urns
        the color of Aleppo honey, superb.
Price: £200, negotiable.

        Cromartie
        Sutherland-Leveson-Gower's
agitated neighbors claim
the whole entombed estate's due
for demolition in the spring,
        but you can own a piece
        of real pastoral history
before the pleasure grounds
        are razed, a reminder
        of life's improved
        and still-improving things.

II.

Abandoned by the Duke
because the pent-up River Trent
        ran dark with sewage,
        the former priory
        sits servantless, a gassed hive,
just another lost house that won't sell.
Even put up, free of charge,
        to Stoke-on-Trent
        and Staffordshire,
        its belvedere tower

Advertisement, Architectural Supplement to Country Life

double-locks with mold.
Will no one come to tour?

III.

Only the royal deer-park
proves eternal. Families
of fallow deer serpentine
        through the old shooting gallery
        of oaks. They have the run
        of it now, each occluded barrow,
every hedgerow stretching out
forever, the blackcurrants
that the children used to gather,
        back when there were children here.

Animal, Vegetable, Mineral

Unlike your lowbrow friends, you've got good taste.
You like the right things: Mahler; Hockney; Lowell.
You know your diamonds from your diamond paste;

your citrine's brilliant-cut, not double-faced;
you've never gulped your rose-flecked finger bowl,
unlike your bourgeois peers. You've got real taste.

Your fondness for Quimper might be misplaced,
but not your love of sterling straws or tole.
You know your rubies from your ruby paste.

You list, at length, lost colleagues you've replaced
for giving you a faux Pashmina stole,
hair brooch, scotched eau-de-vie. *Charm's trumped by taste*,

you sigh. So rustic mobs think you're straight-laced?
You polish fruit knives, not your gilt-leaf soul.
You know freshwater pearls from vintage paste.

Your fescue, cropped by sheep, is poppy-laced,
a verdure unimpaired by labored mole.
You've joined the Hunt Club. Your accent's long-erased.
You know your Early Girls from your tomato paste.

Homewood, 1816

You have to leave him, Harriet, and soon.
Before he drains the cellarette. Before
the pier glass warps. Forget the cherry demi-lune—

you have to pack the plate and lock the door,
dismiss Miss Ware and Master Deal. You need
to keep your children safe as saints. He'll take it sore;

I know Charley—sober, drunk, he'll plead
his cogent case, then crowd the monteith bowl
with chiseled ice. It's you who bled four times, who bleeds;

who pays for every pilaster and pole,
chintz tassels, trompe l'oeil, medallions, swag—
not with your landed dowry, but your mousetrap soul.

So long as you seek freedom, fold the flag;
swap red silk drapes for tattered lunar blue;
keep greenbacks hidden in your rose hip carpetbag.

Refuse his apologia, and, too,
his chemic bed; imported marzipan,
black Running Diamond sailcloth, mock-jade knives; each new

print, violet gown, or walrus scrimshaw fan.
I'm cutting off his yearly grant; my son
will not "improve," like ale, with time. A sorry man,

rum-dissipated heir—his life half-done,
his fortune squandered, all his business null.
Dear Harriet, I know that you were fairly won—

your love-match dazzled us. But charm's his hull;
raw wit obscures the bitter nut. It's time
to leave. The harvest moon grows streaky, gibbous, dull.

Homewood, 1816

I am an old man, not a fool, and in my prime
I was a founding father. Let me father you.
Your lemon house will sweet with tangerine and lime;
your ruby life will facet, sheared: a rose quartz chime.

The Last Country House

Digum Laude Virum Musa Vetat Mori

I lost her in the maze at Hampton Court
    beside a bottomless reflecting pool.
Through edged parterres, beyond the tennis court,
    a pleached lime passage glinted, quickset, cool.

I searched the Grotto, the Illusion Cove,
    the Cave of Skeletons, moist hothouse panes.
A topiary rabbit loomed; the Grove
    of Lantern Slides was slit with bamboo canes.

Why did I build the Chinese Kiosk (lit
    by fireflies), the Orangery Dome?
Who visits winter gardens? Who could sit
    content in ruined replicas of Rome?

She vanished from the boxwood avenue,
    the hermitage, the Crystal Obelisk.
These pleasure grounds must lack the proper view,
    be too Sublime (or not quite Picturesque?).

No matter; I must tend the waterscape,
    the model Matterhorn's steep Alpine peaks.
For after baccarat, half-blitzed, escape
    is summerhouses, candytufts, antiques.

Food Editor, *Electricity on the Farm* Magazine

Sequestered in her corner office, sans Hudson River
views, she settles up her final IOUs.
A salaried girl, her marriage all but over,

she zips and unzips her own mackerel-gray suit.
She's learned to broil Steak Diane for one
and memorized the West Side Local's thunder.

At night in her low-rent efficiency,
she drafts nut graphs on errant blow-in cards.
Her best reporters—sick of pre-electric farms,

failed fudge cake recipes, and falling revenues—
defect to *Vogue*: *her* fault, she frets. In her *His
Girl Friday* haze, she chain smokes, picturing Rosalind

Russell's set chin and snap-brim comebacks, so unlike
her own engraved commands. Now watch her sift
white sugar superfine, blue pencil snapped

beside the test kitchen's spun-down microwave,
her face a battered pearl. Still drawn, despite
small claims and charms, to work's frail constancy.

Livia da Porto Thiene and Her Daughter Porzia

The mossy daughter, peering out behind
her mother's lynx-lined coat, is safe for now.
It rarely snows in Venice-by-the-Sea.
Flushed mother smoothes rose attar in her hair.
But Livia's distracted gaze—beyond
the frame, past her harsh husband handling his
hard son—is honed and hammer-heavy. Next
year, she'll bleed out in childbirth, the still-

born's skin like Iceland spar. Shy Porzia will
inherit her stiff marten wrap, its death's
head dipped in bony gold; her rusty cloak,
dense winter furs, and fat umbilical pearls;
her swollen, rouge-red gown, like breast milk mixed
with menstrual blood. In ten years' time, she'll have
her mother's rosined beauty, too: black hair
in glossy plaits; eyes bleak as raven's wings.

In ten years' time, her father's gaze will turn,
a compass needle tracking her pale neck.
Her brandied brother, drowned in cups and cards,
won't sober up or leave off whores in time
to save her from that rotting marriage bed,
so she'll stow her diseased trousseau—the dress
run through with summer stars; her molten ring;
that heart-shaped bodice, slashed, damp silk bunched through

its slits like veins—inside a chestnut shell.
One magpie midnight, cloaked in Livia's
moth-eaten fur, her face smudged bear-grease gray,
she'll flee her kingdom for the wild wood.
In fairytales like this, stalked women hide in dens
and ditches, scavenging for rocket, duck
eggs, slivered sunfish, till they find themselves
in foreign lands, or royal hunters flush

Livia da Porto Thiene and Her Daughter Porzia

them out and, laughing at their tawny coats,
give them a place at court—a kitchen job,
deglazing pans or shocking mustard greens;
the mad king's filthy aviary for
a berth. In tales like this, girls fall, first-sight,
for any young, unbearded prince who holds
the throne. They wear dewed satin to the ball
and win his heart, then disappear by dawn.

In tales like this, girls slip a solid ring
inside shark soup—the broth so rich, the ring
so gold, he'll stalk her to the cellar, know,
despite her sweat-streaked face and blistered hands,
it's her. They'll wed, a true love-match—until
she finds him bleeding crows and mourning doves,
or raving, crouched inside his father's grave,
and comes to understand how madness runs

through families like a butcher's knotted twine.
In this tale, though she finds that prince, that court,
she'll find the kitchen warm, the servants stout
and brassy, kinder than she'd known. She'll cut
her hair short (lice) and let her beauty go;
she'll rub her hands raw skinning rabbits, scald
her arms to elbows, burn dry lavender
to mask the scent of hacked beef bones. She'll learn

to stuff raw figs with forcemeat, cure cockscomb,
sweat tender sage; she'll learn to separate
goats' cloudy milk from cream. Her bridal cakes
will taste like rose cachou. There won't be men
who love her quite as meat loves salt, but life's
a white rose nonetheless. One day she'll spot
her father in a crowd of supplicants—
a beggar now, purblind, his falcon face

Livia da Porto Thiene and Her Daughter Porzia

a wrinkled web. Once, Livia was curt
and cold, her dress like ruddy afterbirth;
once, Porzia clung to that unsteady light
like fire moss. They stand together now,
bright, hard as watermelon tourmaline.

Sabbathday Lake

New Gloucester, Maine

You can count the last living Shakers
on one thumbless hand:
two Brethren, Wayne and Arnold,
both farmer-tanned, hair curled up into excelsior;
two Sisters, June and Frances,
their latched throats veined as stewed rhubarb.
Everywhere they go, they shadow each other
from a clapboard distance: two virgins scale the men's staircase,
two virgins stumble down the women's staircase.

Celibacy tastes like the cold cedar rapids
that feed each antique gristmill.
There are never any lasting converts.
Each novice-in-waiting hitchhikes back to Boston
before the timothy is baled. Most nights,
the Shakers sit around a colicky police scanner,
tipping their ladder-back chairs onto two legs,
hoping to hear, through the cornstarch static,
someone untouched, in trouble, who knows how to press cider.

In the apiary, the Shakers work together
gathering soul-of-flowers honey.
They long to be buried beneath
a single anthracite slab, skulls massed
in a sod grave like a band of stars. They think
about the last Shaker at Canterbury, who lived alone
in a hot, high dormitory with newspapers carpeting
the bathroom floor. She died up there last summer,
curled on an iron cot. Not one of the Shakers
has met the dual-gendered god
or seen Mother Ann conjured out of a forge fire.

The Girl Detective

"So, it's come to that," she said. "You're jealous of policemen."
—Dashiell Hammett, The Thin Man

The girl detective does not date
She sits at home   eating a piece of devil's food cake
with red frosting   She sits at home
with a pregnancy test
    Icebox light   slats the kitchenette

The girl detective rolls seamed stockings down
one at a time, slips   off her crepe de chine
and navy pumps   In dotted swiss pajamas
    she yanks out the lousy Murphy bed
flips on her hot-bulb Hawaiian lamp
    the hula dancer's   pampas skirt sways
    hips like lava   skin like kola nut

The girl detective   sets her honey hair
on frozen orange   juice cans
             She double-checks
her clutch purse   for Sweetheart tweezers, compact, blush
then badge   and gun

    Foundation caramelizes   in her vanity mirror
        a bullet lipstick   ricochets
across the room   The girl detective dreams
of handcuffs   slanted grillwork
lost keys and prison   movies where the girls
    are Lana Turner blond

    All her exes broke
the law   or moved to Hollywood
in search of starlets   sunglass swimming pools
palm trees   and palisades
    green velvet theatres sinking   into mossy film noir

The girl detective   keeps a corkscrew handy
things always do go south   it's best to be prepared

Winter Quarters: Cleveland, 1960

"Things are not going well."
—Weldon Kees, "When the Lease Is Up"

Weldon Kees is not dead, only missing. My Plymouth,
abandoned at the Golden Gate, keys jammed
      in the startled ignition,
was a decoy. Like Ambrose Bierce, I escaped the fogged
Embarcadero; I flew Pan Am to Cleveland, paying cash in advance
      for Johnny Weissmuller's old suite at the Alcazar Hotel.

Alone, I dined on scotch and Higbee muffins at the Silver Grille.
Days, I dozed beneath the skylight-bruising lemon tree
      at the Rockefeller Greenhouse;
nights, I rattled down Euclid Avenue, peering into the boarded-up
estates on Millionaire's Row, the moon a pool of lager.
      Cleveland's winter

was one long black-out, Lake Erie a veal chop, pounded thin.
Some *Cleveland Press* cub reporter might, I dreamt, discover
      that *Mr. Kees is a real Clevelander now,*
flat, asthmatic, reluctant, standard. Today, a bird—all red, clutching
a gold seed in its beak—beat its sharp head against my hotel window.
      A pendant of blood

boiled on the frosted glass. I put "Sweet Substitute"
on the record player and forced open an ice-cold can
      with a church key.
No one knows why Weldon Kees has vanished from the Golden State
and struck out for Cuyahoga County in weatherizing season, but
      he is here for the long haul.

Charm City

The dusty Palm Court Palisade shut down
in August '52. Reopened, roped
off, rouged, as Ruby Lounge in '66:

a Rat Pack–era dive, tobacco-cured.
Stacked, star-struck call girls paced the cake tier stage
or lounged for lurid stills on buckshot silk;

magicians mingled, swapping riddled card
tricks; and thin vaudevillian spinsters shuffled off
to barren Buffalo. On swampy, tent

revival Sunday nights, a sibling pair
of brawny Cuban acrobats launched pie
plates through the sequined air, then, glazed with curl

wax, turned back handsprings, juggled jagged shivs,
spun flaming hula hoops. The joint went fish
egg up next Halloween—illegal bus

boys, bums, and borscht-belt jokesters hustled out
to Fells or Pimlico; cut cardsharps soaked
in Natty Boh; docks dank with Can Co. fog.

From Druid Hill to tony Roland Park,
past Waverly, slick Mobtown slid down, roughed,
a low-watt chorus girl in kitten heels.

The wormwood Oak Bar leased for dismal Sweet
Sixteens. On 1st and Park, the Starland Strand—
sleet-battered, boarded up, its mirror globe

a wrecking ball, that sagging balcony
where Billie Holiday swooned "Trav'lin' Light,"
gardenias stick-pinned through her smoky curls—

Charm City

collapsed, worn tap shoes pounding in the pit,
a bare bulb noosed and swinging by the steel
plate fire door, torch-gutted dressing rooms.

The crenellated Belvedere corrodes;
the Coffee Pot fades out like powdered milk,
though Deb and Dot (the hot lunch counter girls)

blacked all the panes with slabbed shoe polish years
ago. The prim Industrial Exchange
survives: skinned coconut ambrosia, ice

cube hearts stained maraschino red. Uptown,
Mount Royal's carved triumphal arch looms like
the tunnel to some Love Canal that lurks

below the rat-trap streets. Cicadas swarm
and breed like rank suburbanites. Old Dime
Museum stubs and geek show tokens nest

inside a patent leather clutch. Back at
the Ruby Lounge, a stripper stops the band
mid-bump and sighs "Strange Fruit" into the hot

box microphone, her eyes like prunes. Night falls;
the audience, that motley crew of thieves
and moneyed Guilford skeletons, drifts off.

At night, each alleyway and oyster skip
shines Judas silver. A sailor's stifled moan
hangs sideways like an off-off-Broadway moon.

The Trial

Circuit Court of Baltimore City

We're here—allegedly—
about a whiskey drunk
whose pick-up clipped a cop
outside the New! Five Mile House.
Because he doesn't testify,
we scrutinize his gut
and blood-drop pinkie ring.
He naps. We nap, or annotate

last Friday's notes; we squint
to read his bitten smirk.
The courtroom's marble, white
as lard, if lard were plinthed. The State's
stilettos do not fit. She rests.
Her closing arguments
unfold like mercury:
a mangled pair of duty pants;

a fat man boneless as
a fifth of gin. The court-
appointed lawyer drawls
"Sometimes, an accident is just
an accident." *So what's a black-
out, then?* I think. *The moon
conspiring to shrink macadam
to a suspect diagram?*

Upstairs, sequestered in
our legal garret with
the medical report (cocaine),
we're forced to cut our knuckles on
the mystery of starlit hit-
and-runs. We won't be good,
or kind, or just, just us.
Dead quiet, deadlocked, putting up

The Trial

a fuss. Please, bailiff, tell
our spare obstructionist
the truth: not all police
collude, but Beaux-Arts murals lie.
The law is linseed mixed with dust.
We want apology,
and, next time, doing right.
But everything's redacted—smudged.

We exit into St. Paul's endless night.

Letter from Algiers Naval Station, Louisiana

The life is pretty good down here.
A guy can buy a nickel beer
and 10-inch strings of smoked boudin,
or eat price fix with dress whites on
in New Orleans's best lobster joint.

The C.O. decided to appoint
me to the Brig from Shore Patrol.
I'm busting guys who go AWOL;
censoring postcards prisoners write,
guarding lockjaw cells at night—

feels almost like I'm back in Vice.
The Gulf civilians treat us nice;
most officers are friendly, too.
Nobody hassles me, lone Jew
on board the carrier.

                            It's dark
tonight, but for the match and spark
of sailor's cigarettes. Back from
the dance, some shots, a girl—hot sum
of all their dreams—they lean back, joke.
The sea is turning, black as smoke,
in countries none of us have seen.

Jughead, Mid-Life

In Tokyo, the long dream of Riverdale fades
        like spilled Hitachino Nest. Who was I back then?
Seventeen, my stomach an empty eel,
        no eye for women. I knew my way around
a short sheet. I knew Big Ethel's tears
        must taste like celery salt, and what
the secret *S* stood for on my ringer T,
        and how to bang out "Sex and Candy" on a drum kit.

Eyes shut—some dumb mystic—I could predict
        whether a random tin can buoyed SPAM, or chaw,
or licorice Altoids. But high school ended,
        and everybody scattered. Even Archie lost
his knack for wise-ass love triangles. At Oberlin,
        I found, the food was infinite, and infinitely bad:
grease-trap soft-serve; gristled albumen. I slept through
        Pornography: Writing of Prostitutes. I slept

through everything, until they didn't ask me back.
        And that was it for me. I mean, I lost my appetite
for Rutt's Hut rippers, fake IDs, and *Philadelphia Story*.
        My cut-up beanie, badged with stars. My belief,
that pure Americana, that anything could be finagled.
        Now, I make my way past love hotels
and rabbit cafés, one hapless ex-pat among
        the salarymen. The subway smells like cut salami.

Is this Japan, or just an afterlife where nobody
        likes cheese? Every pal I knew back then
is bankrupt, mortgaged, or screwing someone
        on the side. Their kids have eyes as tight as ticks.
So I couldn't face the entropy of growing up.
        Here, I might be strange, but at least
the sunsets flame like diesel gasoline
        and the noodles are all hand-pulled, alkaline.

Jughead, Mid-Life

It tastes good, is what I'm saying. Like gold.
        Salt-packed, uncomplicated
as a demo reel. I still don't know
        what turns a woman's buckwheat gaze,
but I can melt pork bones
        into *tonkatsu* broth, and I've learned
some breakaway Japanese. Unbroken pleasure's
        larded like *kae-dama*. It's a soft-cooked egg.

Dust Bowl: The Advance Man's Geography

I travel solo, railway town to town,
a single man advancing like a scout,
my luggage crammed with circus lithographs,
a gazetteer inscribed inside my head.

I plaster one-horse burgs and county seats
with blown-up color one-sheets, row on row,
billboarding dry goods walls two weeks before
the Hagenbeck-Wallace spikes a high-grass lot.

I know each boarding house and inn from Rome
to Baraboo; I know which manager
to grease to get the showman's rate, which tea-
room serves half-shells and beef *en croûte* for two.

In better days, I ran a burly crew:
three dozen billpost roustabouts aboard
an iron railroad car named Thunderclap.
But trouble dogged the show. The Wabash Flood

drowned half the elephants and jungle cats;
a locomotive wreck near Ivanhoe
charred eighty-six performers to the bone.
These days, our advertising budget zilch,

I cross bluegrass and glaciate plateaus,
alone save for a company of clowns
and strong men, acrobats in oil crayon.
Most villages are starlit ghost towns now.

I paste the posters up on burnt-out barns;
black blizzards try to tug them from my hands.
It's lonesome work, but here I am, one man,
the plumb-line prairie ground to hardpan dust.

Sideshow Banner:
The Engagement of the Fat Lady and the Pocket Man

Jacques played my love-struck contract dwarf in tents
from Brou to San-Maur-des-Fossés.
He brought me *saucisson*, champagne,
and Gerber daisies wrapped in cellophane;

he stroked the triple strand of pearls that ringed
my clotted custard double-chin
so tenderly, I almost thought
his sawdust-kneed proposal was sincere.

The banner painter captured our romance
on canvas. There I sit, enthroned
on gilt aluminum, my teeth
bared in a fox-trap grin, my dimpled bulk

blown up to fill a wincey sideshow wall,
forever fat, just twenty-two.
The joke was that a gentleman
that small could fall for someone oversized

and listing, like an alpine *île flottante*,
our false long looks some mastodon mistake.
I fed him *tarte tatin,* marceled my hair,
and kissed his biscuit porcelain brow,

but when the tour closed, he pocketed
my Carbanado diamond ring
and caravanned to Bruges with Snake Charm Elle.
These days, although the cook-tent steams

with *boudin blanc,* I find it hard to put
on weight. Bereft, I slouch beneath
our faded courtship scene, my heart
a punched-in bladder on a birch-bark stick.

Showman with Performing Bear in the Westerwald

August Sander, 1929

He pinned the bear in a foothold trap
one summer, a lone cub the color of rye bread
caught pawing through the trash
outside Kreutz's butcher shop.

The showman pierced its nose with a steel ring.
He taught it to balance
a cube of smoked pork belly
on its tender snout, and how to puff

on a pipe packed with talcum powder.
He dipped its paws in a tin of Vaseline
and made it stand on a red-hot iron plate—
this is how it learned to waltz like a man, on two legs.

Here, the beast squats beside the showman,
not pulling on its knotted chain,
patient, while an itinerant photographer
takes their portrait picture.

The showman, picking
his gums with a rasp, boasts
Bruno adjusted quickly to his muzzle.
He does not tell the photographer

about the teeth he wrenched out, one by one,
bone-shearing carnassials, with a pair
of tongue-and-groove pliers,
the giant's maw collapsing in on itself,

or how he washed and combed
the bear's blood-matted fur
until each hair stiffened and shone,
almost smotheringly tender.

Showman with Performing Bear in the Westerwald

Instead, he complains about
the butcher's stingy daughter, her braid
as thick as *dopplebock*. These days,
every stunner is a secret Jew.

Epiphany. The banks are failing
in Berlin. At night, the showman dreams
of his performing bear, grown
to its full ten feet. How marvelous

his bristling fur will look then. How huge
his gold-melting claws. The Fatherland
spreads out around their tent, a blistered tapestry.
All of Germany is ready for them now.

Fat Man

This larded fat's no £5 barrow swine:
like Barnum's sperm whales, blubber boiled in brine,
his salt-packed ham hocks weigh a quarter ton.
His gut churns, Globe of Death or smoked pork bun;
the clutch jaw in his suckling skull's unhinged.
Greased, adiposean, but barely singed
when P. T.'s curios went up in flame—
tusked waxworks split; king cannibal courts maimed;
those sperm whales blistered in their rendering tanks—
Big's brisket muscles, buttered heart to flanks,
chilled like the cold cream lining of a fox
fur wrap. Too clot to hug. Lugged off, a Bock's
Car bomb. Pitched like a pack of magic, Big
blots Nagasaki. Flying fetal pig
or fetid sumo, not a Trinity
test Gadget, but a warhead-slash-divinity,
slick sideshow Buddha, last Fat Man on Earth
or in the Milky Way with planetary girth.

Atomograd

Atom City, Ukraine

I. Prypiat Funfair

The locked Ferris wheel arcs
against the horizon,

a honey fungus
flexing its golden gills.

Suspended
from petrified cogs,

the cars seed
the ash trees below

with powdered rust.
Beeswax capsules

loft through dead air
like irradiated spores.

II. Worm Wood Forest

A plume of light
leached sphagnum moss
from the cold bark
of the nuclear forest.

The oak groves steamed;
the black alders flushed ginger.
Hornbeams grew gigantic,
roots and trunks coiling like double yolks.

Each thorny pine, each saxifrage
and small-flowered bitter,
was bulldozed and buried
in a vast fen grave.

The half-life soil
silvered
under its cargo
of nettled atoms;
a corncrake quarried
the fissured stream
for pike, its beak
a carpenter's rasp.

III. The Pier

Patched barges sluice sideways
into the phosphorescent river,

their bellies black bison,
scabbed with radiation.

The barge captains evacuated
long ago, pressure-dazed, slipping

through the alienation zone
like wild boar. What remains, now:

cucumber shoots drilling
the greenhouse glass, storks

nesting in the melted reactor,
the schoolhouse a wreck of scalded textbooks,

Atomograd

everywhere the quivering taste
of pins, as if a hedgehog quilled with aluminum

had invaded the dusty samovars
of each sealed concrete tenement.

The barges wait some final passage
like latten ferries embedded in the River Styx.

Paradise

Stan Hywet Hall, est. 1915

Sometimes early morning air
turns the exact shade of rosemary
as you stand at your window looking out
onto the reflecting pool—
this water limed with fallen laurel leaves—
and hearing the deliberate breath of rain
fill the garden with the sound of threshing light,
seeing blackbirds rising,
the stone locket of their beaks,
their igneous feathers,
into a cedar forest
far beyond the whale spines
of snow-banked automobiles,
the languid spires
of manor house and arbor,
casting pale shadows
over the corn crush of Akron fields.

You could travel this world forever
and never know the love of one woman,
or the forgotten meaning of relics,
or even the names of animals foreign to you.
You could search this globe
for the shard-spark
in the hurricane jar,
coming no closer to knowledge
than to the body of your own grief.

But on these mornings
frail as language, when the house casts
its grave bulk over the lawn,
the world of men with its brief roses
and its fear of ice waxes over,
is nothing,
becomes nothing to you.

Paradise

There are only birches   figs   writing paper
tiger mussels   moonrise skimming Portage Path
your father's miniature pagodas,
your own fevered hands caught
under spring's witch hazel light,
these streams grown opalescent
as the map of a young girl's skin,
and knowing that the cold
is still coming
is not yet over,
frost pearled on the lavender,
and that this world is a place of night.

A Note About the Author

Photograph: © Michael Levy Photography

Hilary S. Jacqmin was born in Boston, Massachusetts and grew up in Shaker Heights, Ohio. She earned her BA from Wesleyan University, her MA from the Writing Seminars at Johns Hopkins University, and her MFA from the University of Florida. She lives in Baltimore, Maryland, where she is an editor at Johns Hopkins University Press. Her work has appeared in *Painted Bride Quarterly*, *PANK*, *Best New Poets*, *DIAGRAM*, *FIELD*, and elsewhere.

Other Books from Waywiser

POETRY
Austin Allen, *Pleasures of the Game*
Al Alvarez, *New & Selected Poems*
Chris Andrews, *Lime Green Chair*
George Bradley, *A Few of Her Secrets*
Geoffrey Brock, *Voices Bright Flags*
Robert Conquest, *Blokelore & Blokesongs*
Robert Conquest, *Penultimata*
Morri Creech, *Field Knowledge*
Morri Creech, *The Sleep of Reason*
Peter Dale, *One Another*
Erica Dawson, *Big-Eyed Afraid*
B. H. Fairchild, *The Art of the Lathe*
David Ferry, *On This Side of the River: Selected Poems*
Jeffrey Harrison, *The Names of Things: New & Selected Poems*
Joseph Harrison, *Identity Theft*
Joseph Harrison, *Shakespeare's Horse*
Joseph Harrison, *Someone Else's Name*
Joseph Harrison, ed., *The Hecht Prize Anthology, 2005-2009*
Anthony Hecht, *Collected Later Poems*
Anthony Hecht, *The Darkness and the Light*
Jaimee Hills, *How to Avoid Speaking*
Carrie Jerrell, *After the Revival*
Stephen Kampa, *Bachelor Pad*
Rose Kelleher, *Bundle o' Tinder*
Mark Kraushaar, *The Uncertainty Principle*
Matthew Ladd, *The Book of Emblems*
J. D. McClatchy, *Plundered Hearts: New and Selected Poems*
Dora Malech, *Shore Ordered Ocean*
Jérôme Luc Martin, *The Gardening Fires: Sonnets and Fragments*
Eric McHenry, *Odd Evening*
Eric McHenry, *Potscrubber Lullabies*
Eric McHenry and Nicholas Garland, *Mommy Daddy Evan Sage*
Timothy Murphy, *Very Far North*
Ian Parks, *Shell Island*
V. Penelope Pelizzon, *Whose Flesh is Flame, Whose Bone is Time*
Chris Preddle, *Cattle Console Him*
Shelley Puhak, *Guinevere in Baltimore*
Christopher Ricks, ed., *Joining Music with Reason:*
34 Poets, British and American, Oxford 2004-2009
Daniel Rifenburgh, *Advent*
Mary Jo Salter, *It's Hard to Say: Selected Poems*
W. D. Snodgrass, *Not for Specialists: New & Selected Poems*
Mark Strand, *Almost Invisible*

Other Books from Waywiser

Mark Strand, *Blizzard of One*
Bradford Gray Telford, *Perfect Hurt*
Matthew Thorburn, *This Time Tomorrow*
Cody Walker, *Shuffle and Breakdown*
Cody Walker, *The Self-Styled No-Child*
Deborah Warren, *The Size of Happiness*
Clive Watkins, *Already the Flames*
Clive Watkins, *Jigsaw*
Richard Wilbur, *Anterooms*
Richard Wilbur, *Mayflies*
Richard Wilbur, *Collected Poems 1943-2004*
Norman Williams, *One Unblinking Eye*
Greg Williamson, *A Most Marvelous Piece of Luck*
Greg Williamson, *The Hole Story of Kirby the Sneak and Arlo the True*
Stephen Yenser, *Stone Fruit*

Fiction
Gregory Heath, *The Entire Animal*
Mary Elizabeth Pope, *Divining Venus*
K. M. Ross, *The Blinding Walk*
Gabriel Roth, *The Unknowns**
Matthew Yorke, *Chancing It*

Illustrated
Nicholas Garland, *I wish ...*
Eric McHenry and Nicholas Garland, *Mommy Daddy Evan Sage*
Greg Williamson, *The Hole Story of Kirby the Sneak and Arlo the True*

Non-Fiction
Neil Berry, *Articles of Faith: The Story of British Intellectual Journalism*
Mark Ford, *A Driftwood Altar: Essays and Reviews*
Richard Wollheim, *Germs: A Memoir of Childhood*

* Co-published with Picador